Creative Inspirations

Owls

Coloring Book

John Daniel

Published by PUBLISHING COMPANY in 2015
First edition: First printing
Illustrations and design © 2015 Adult Coloring Book J. Kaiwell

allcoloringbook.com

ISBN-13: 978-1530753062
ISBN-10: 1530753066

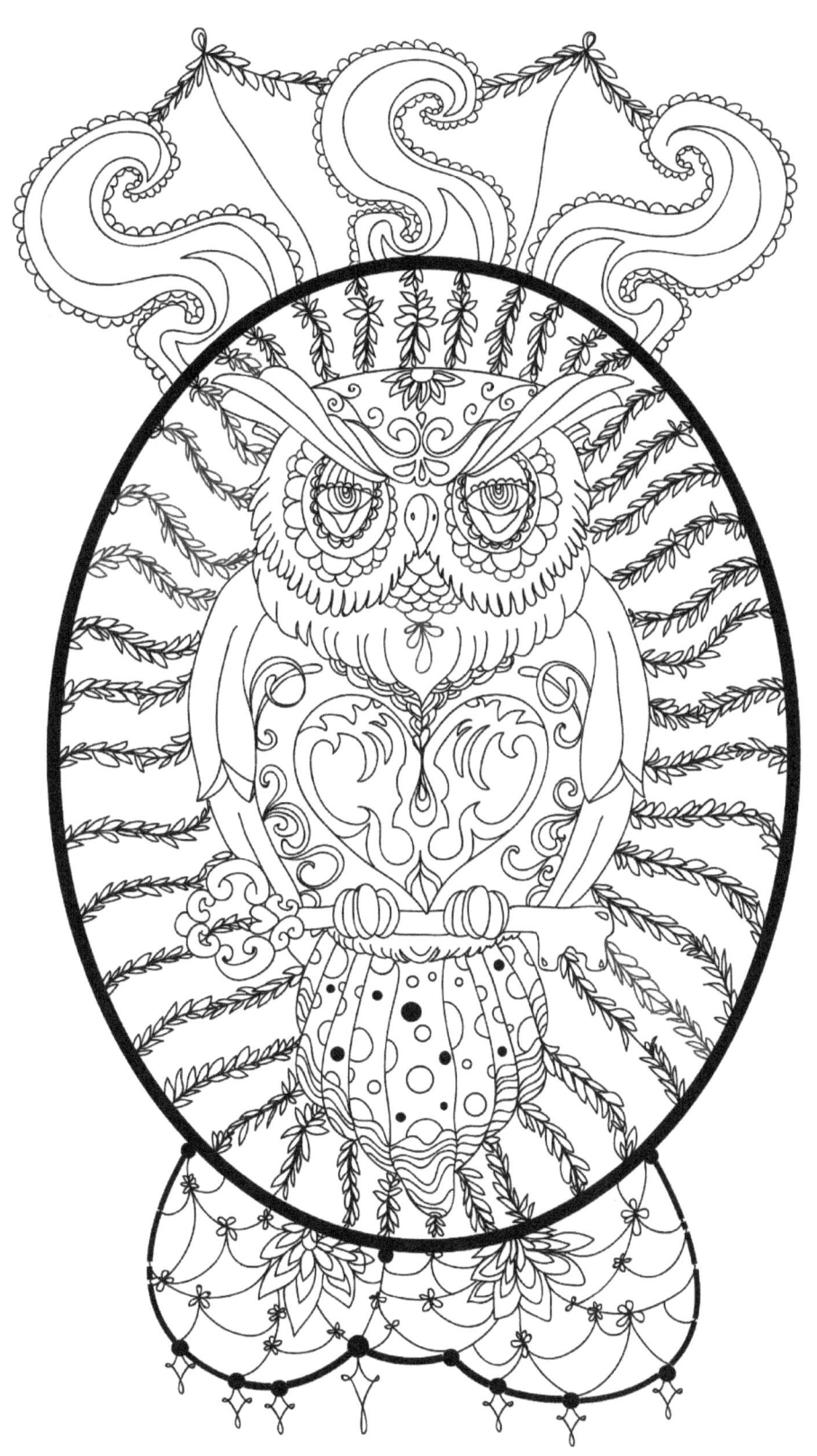

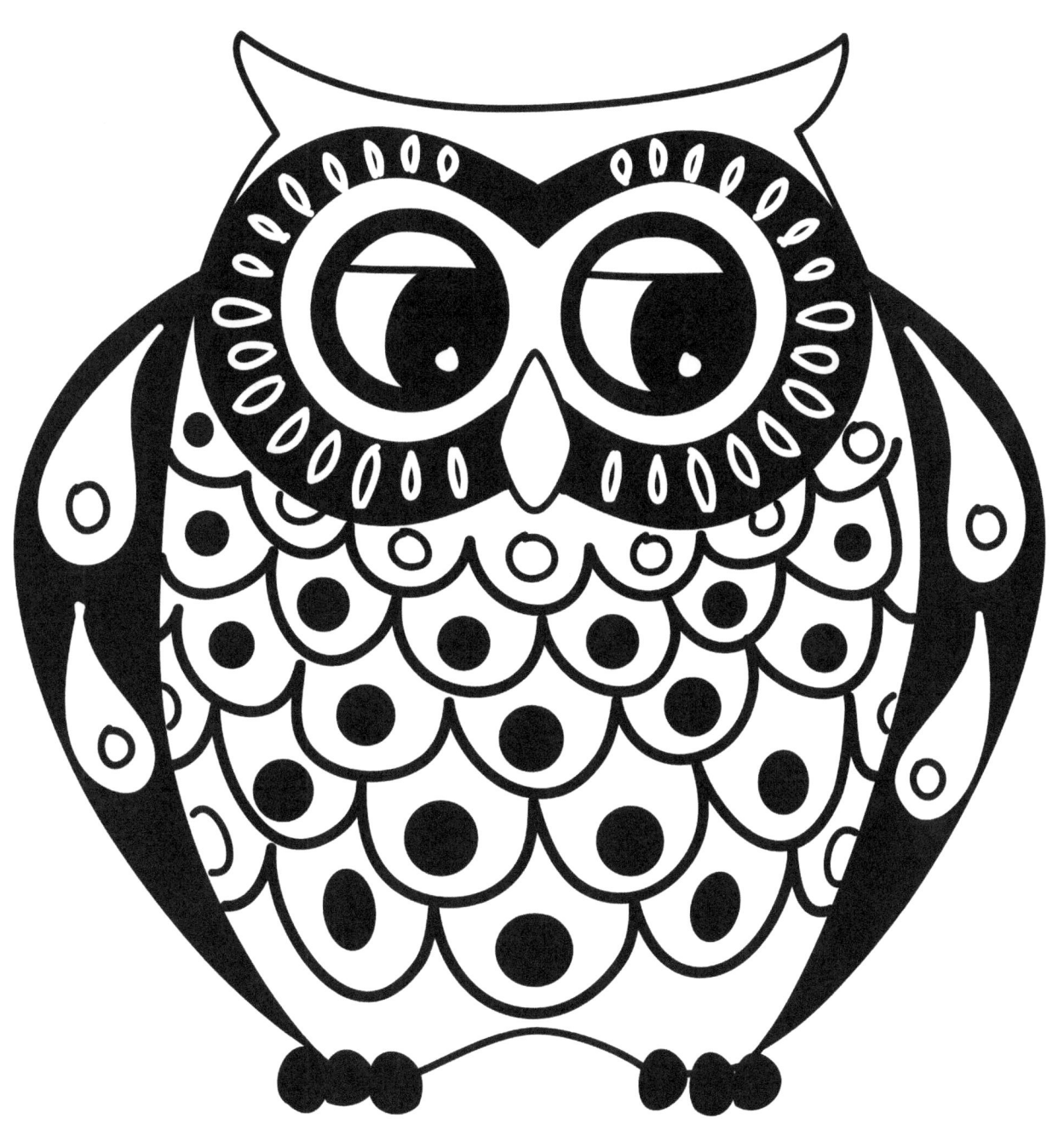

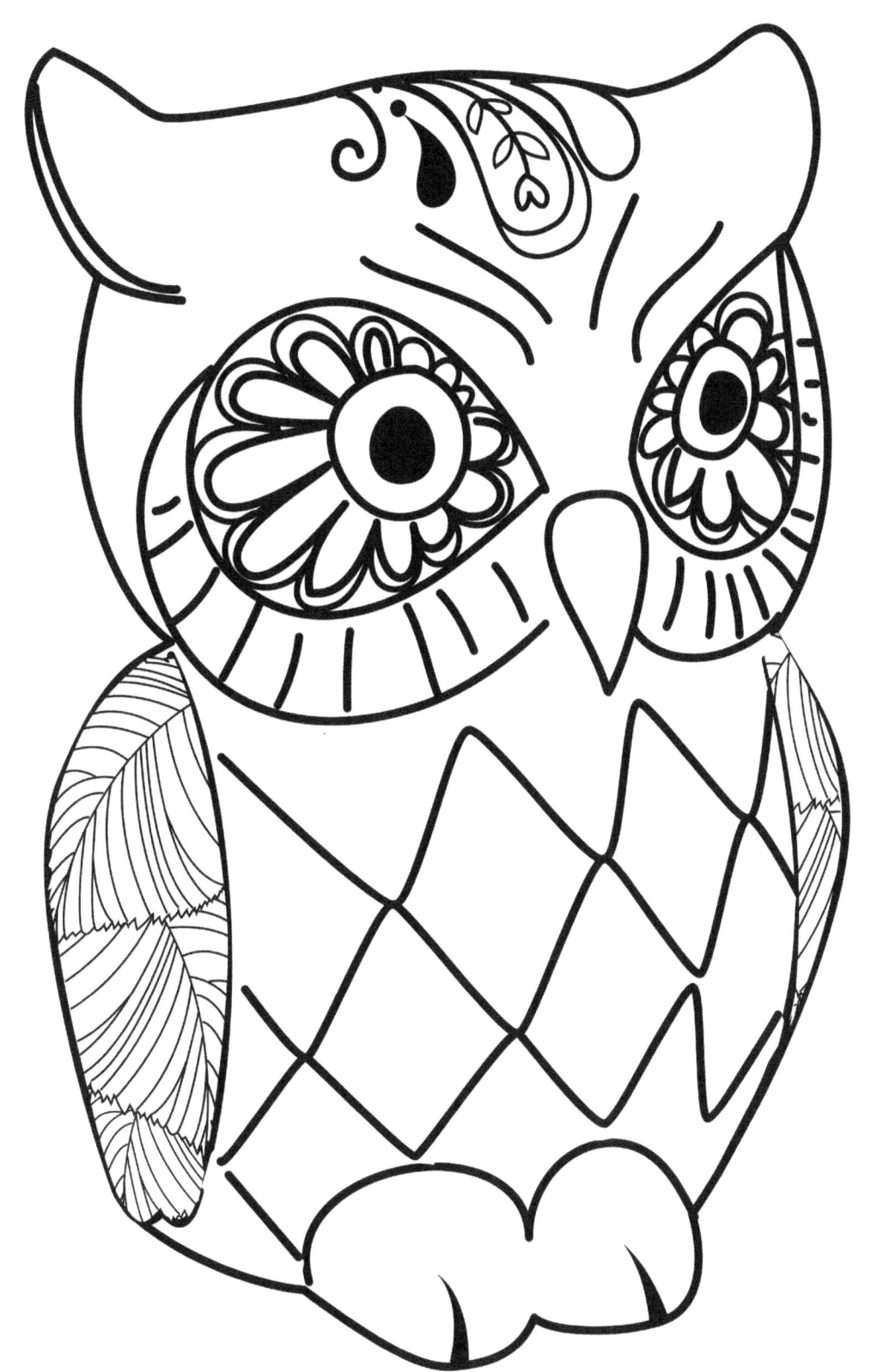

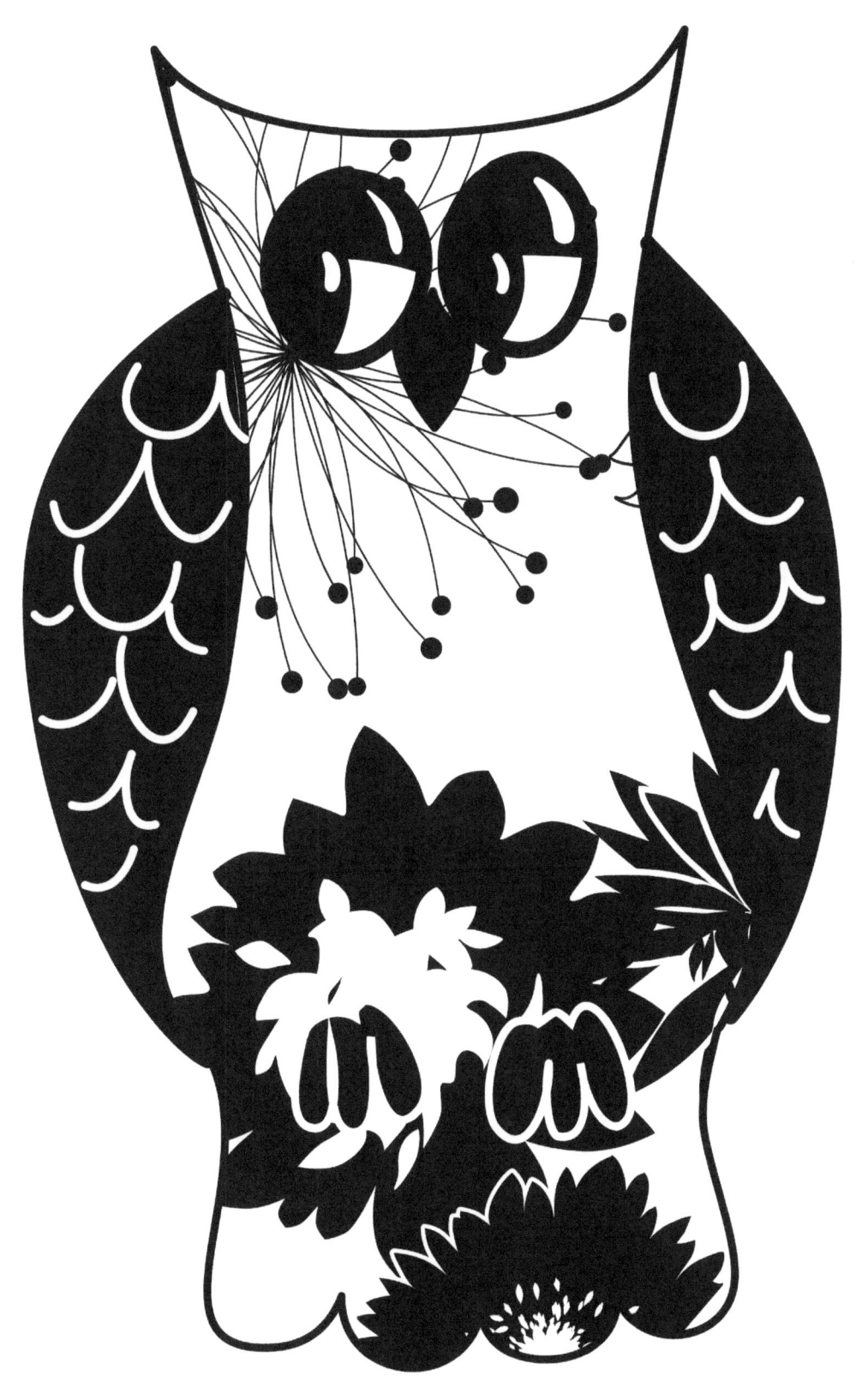

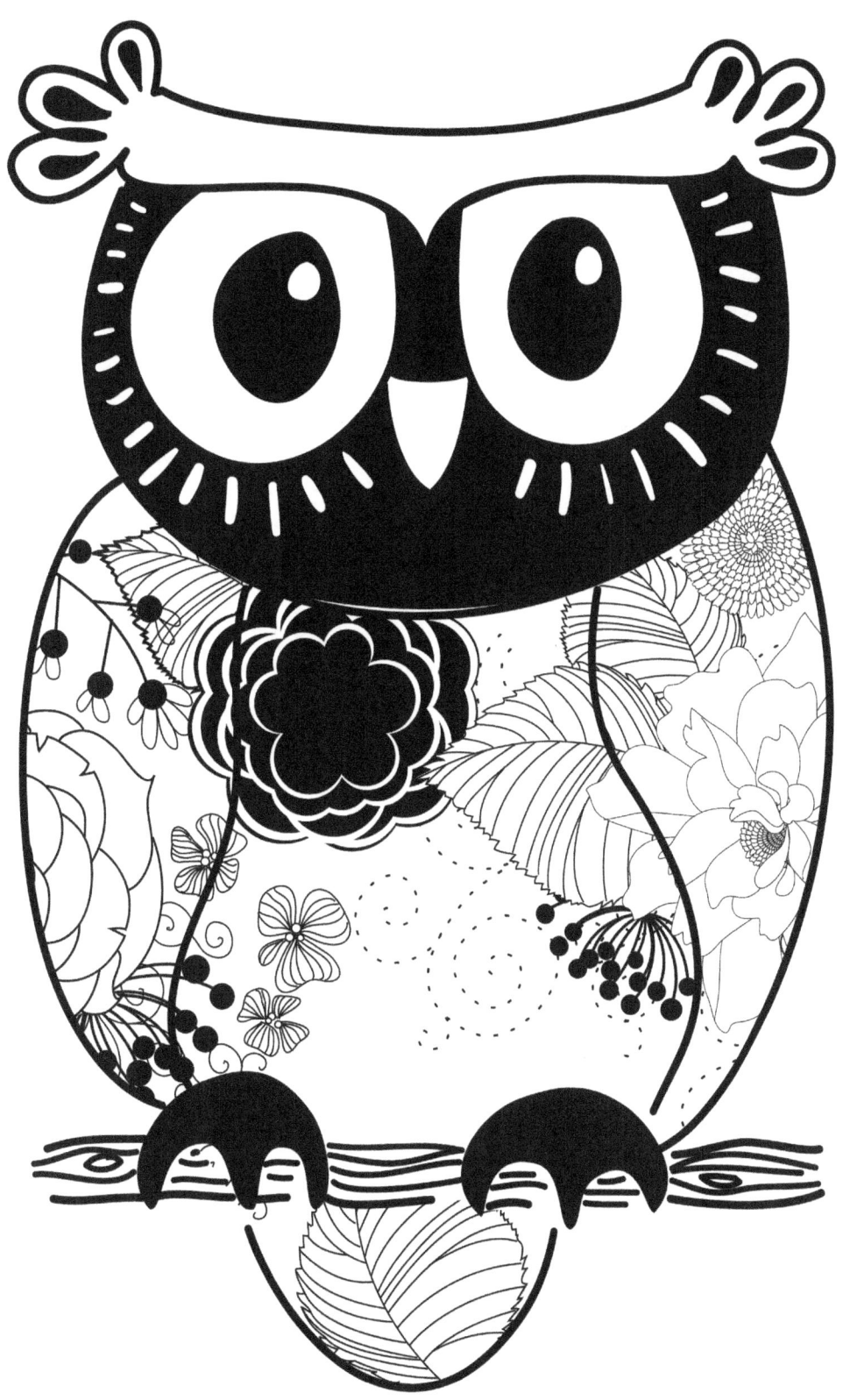

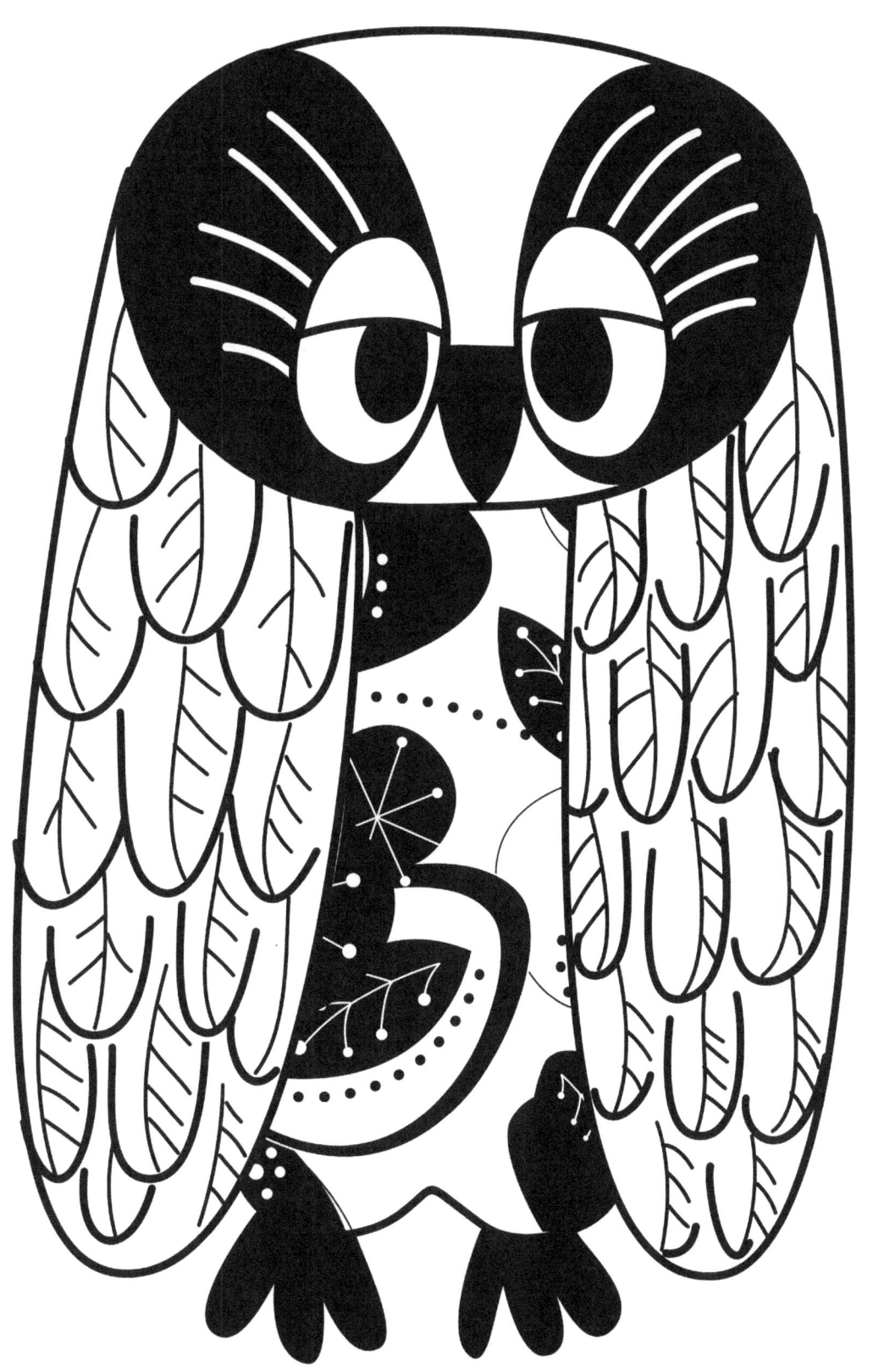

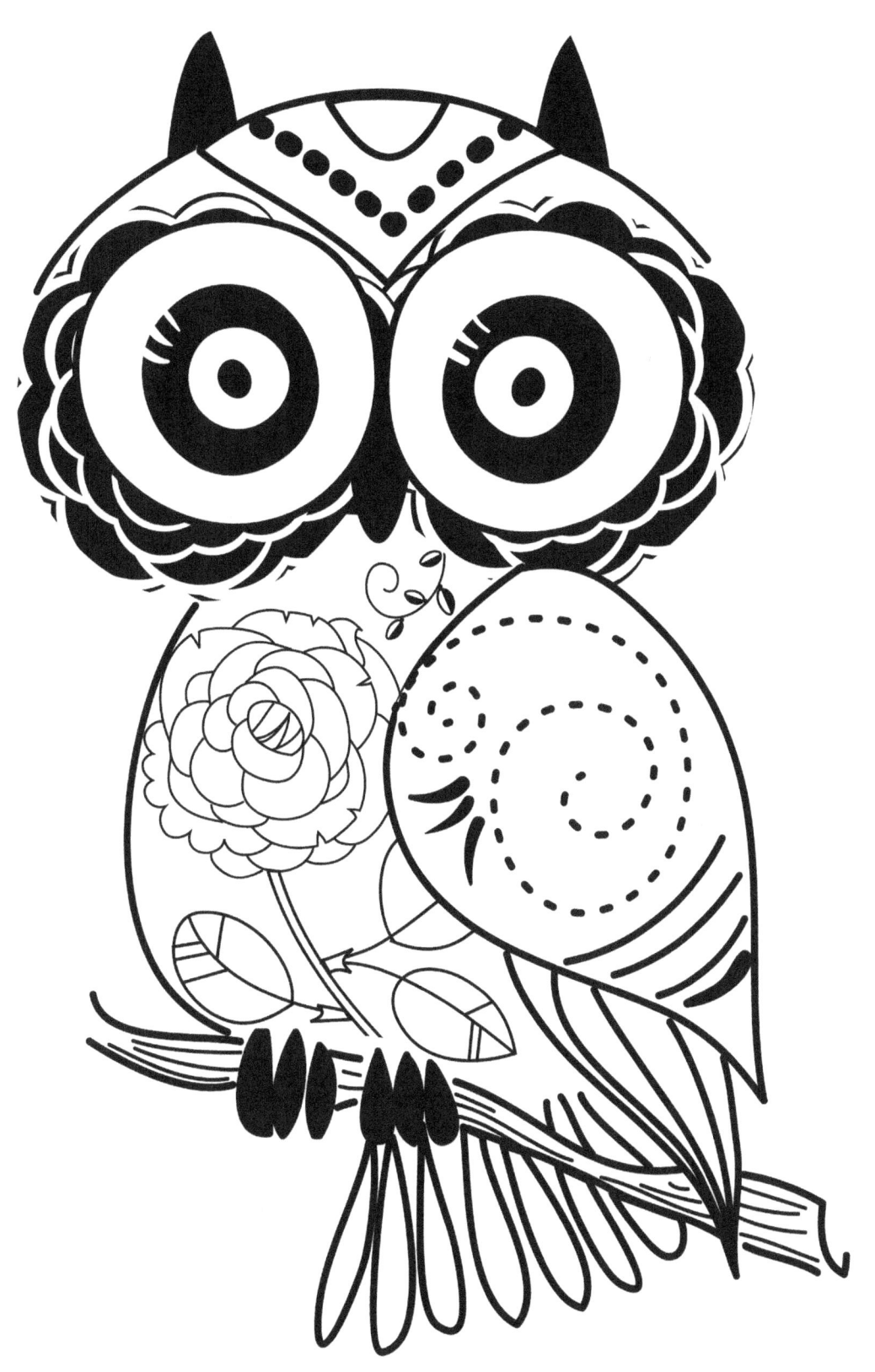

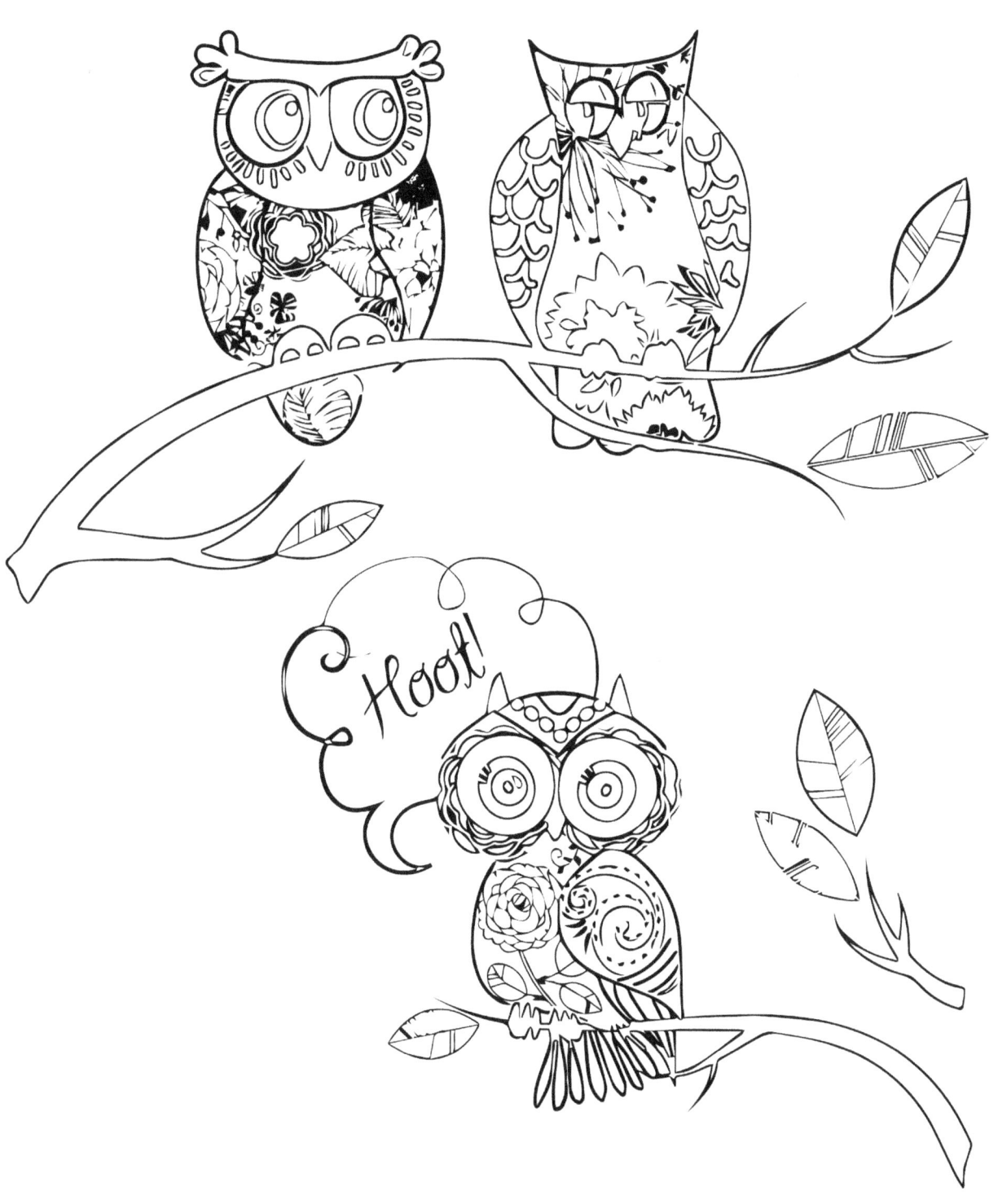

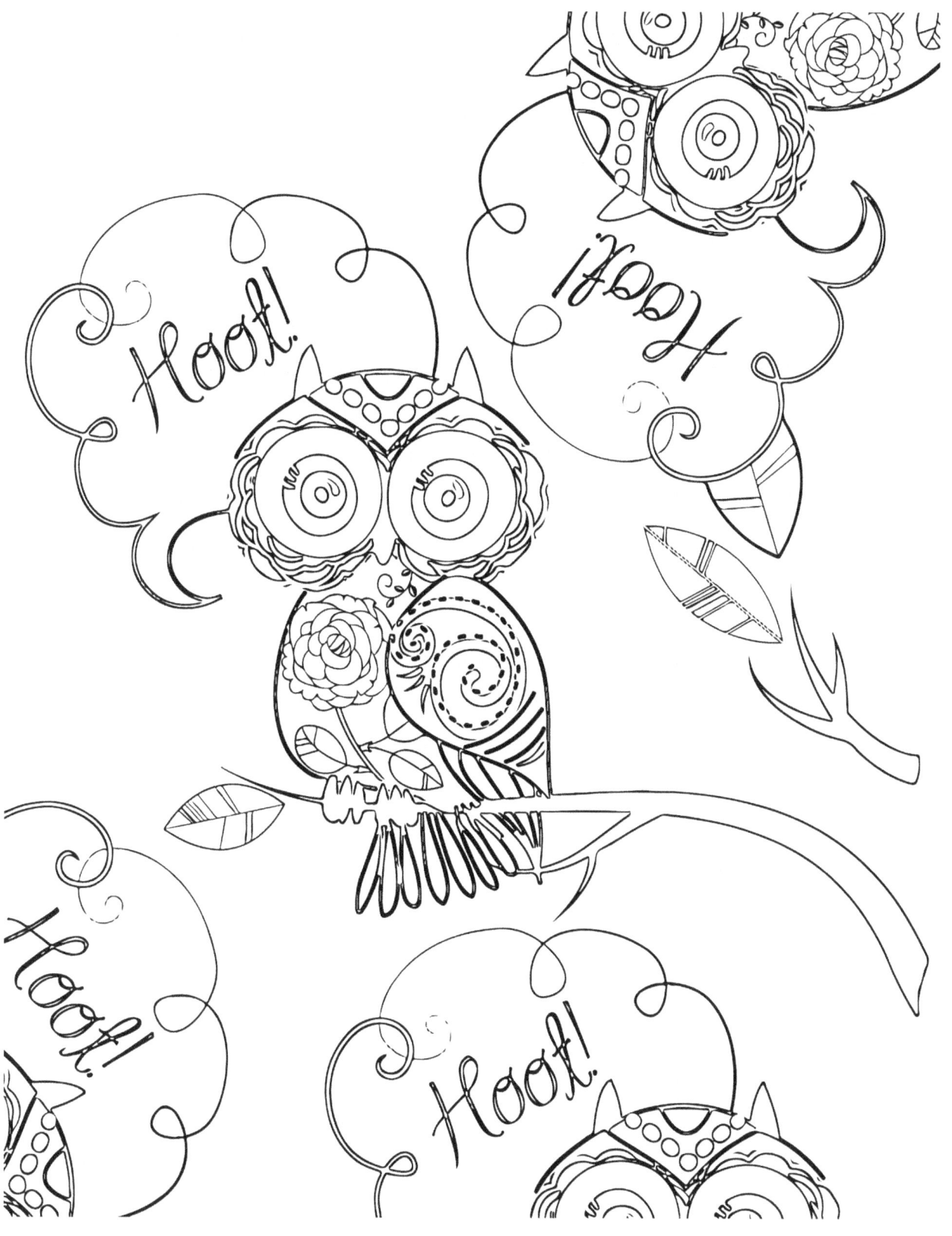

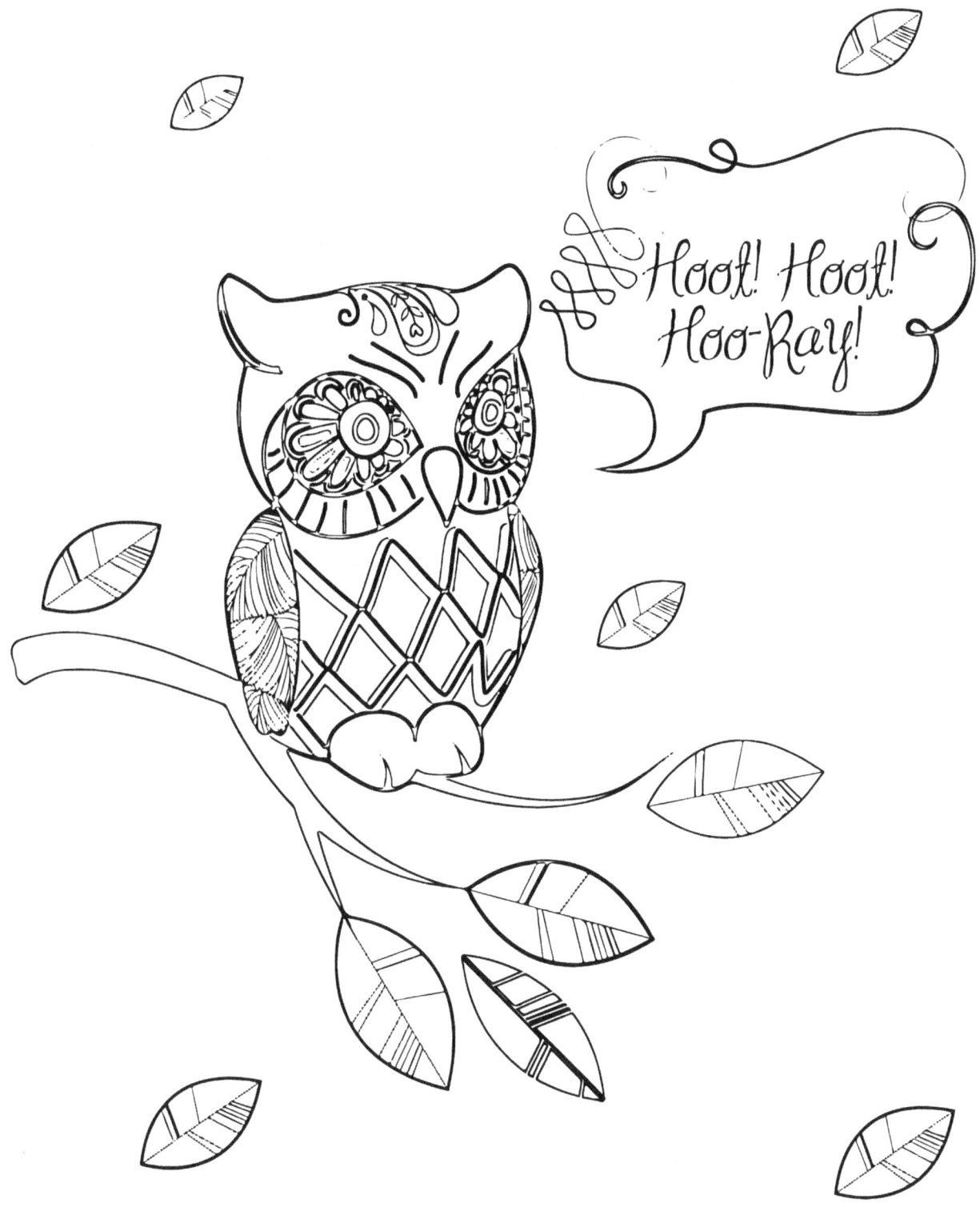

Owls

Owls

HOoooot!

Owls

Owls

Owls

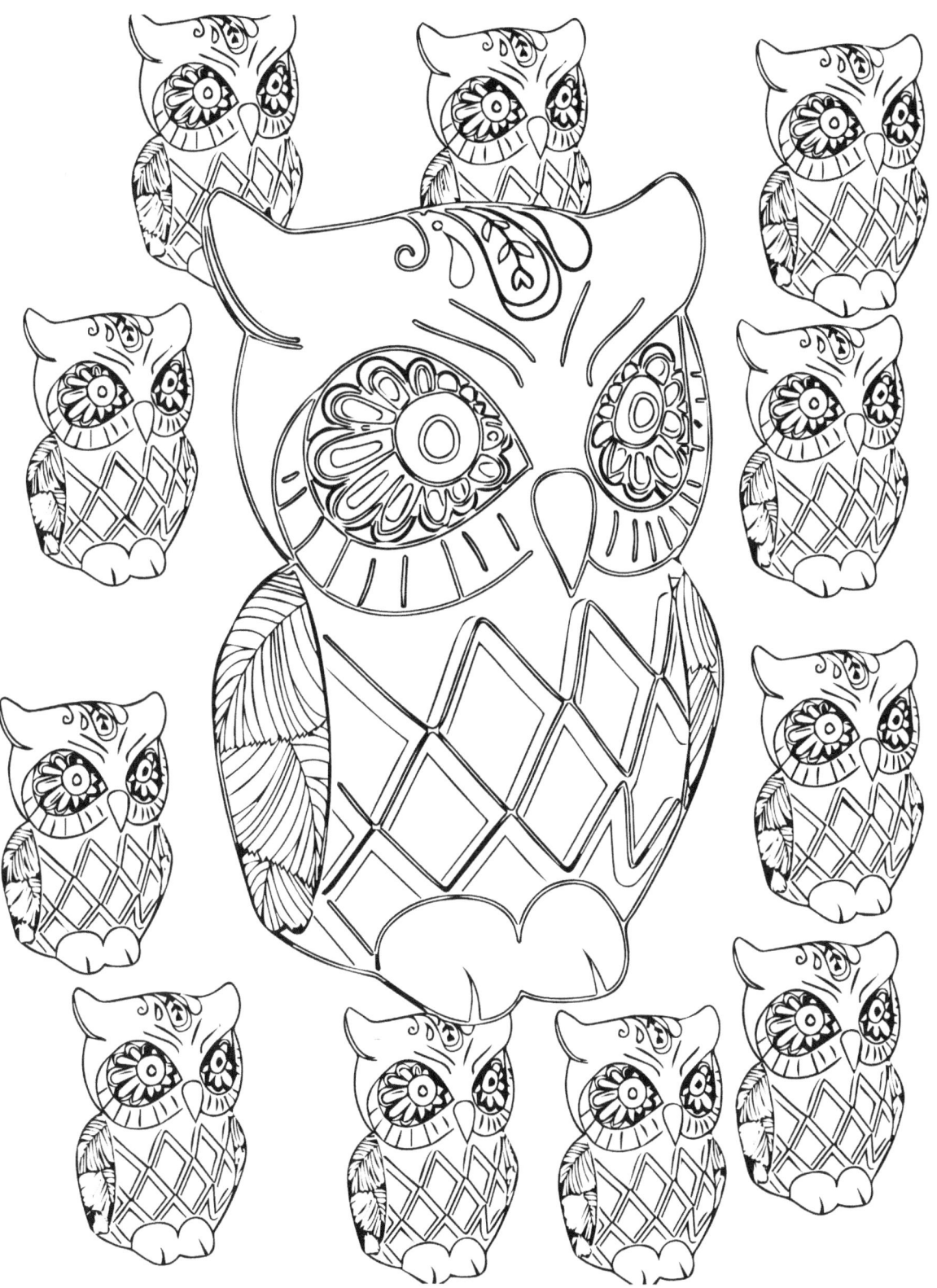

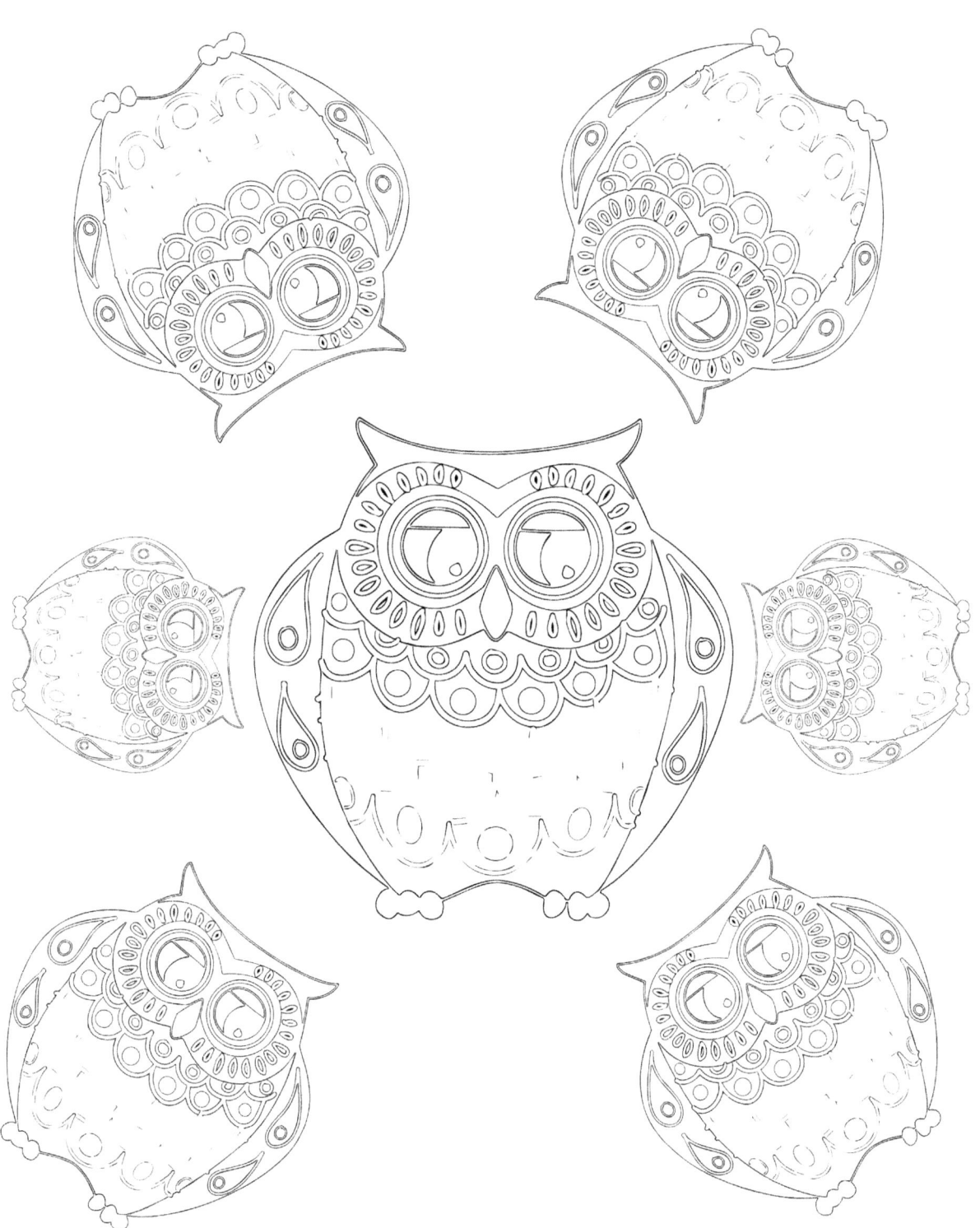

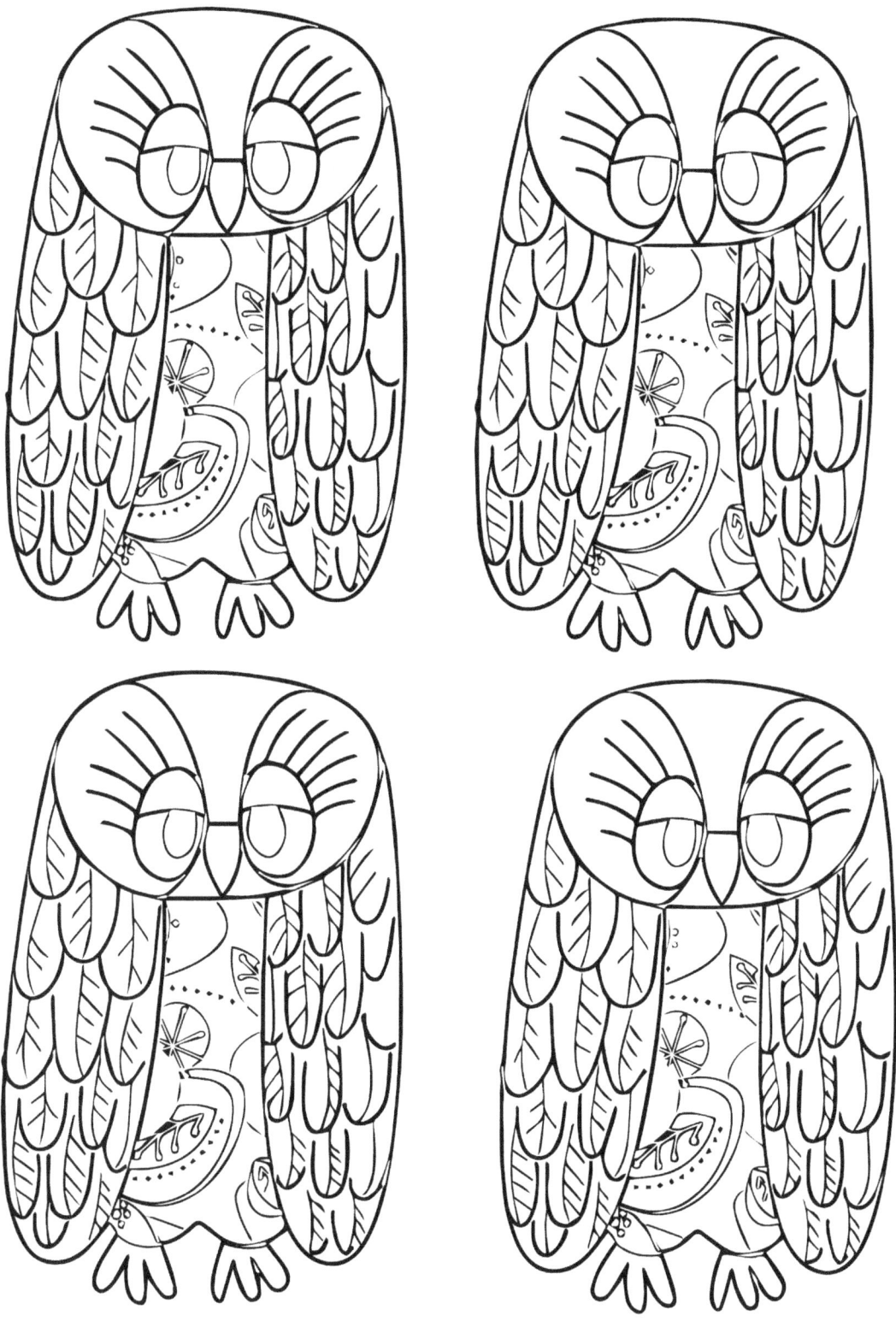

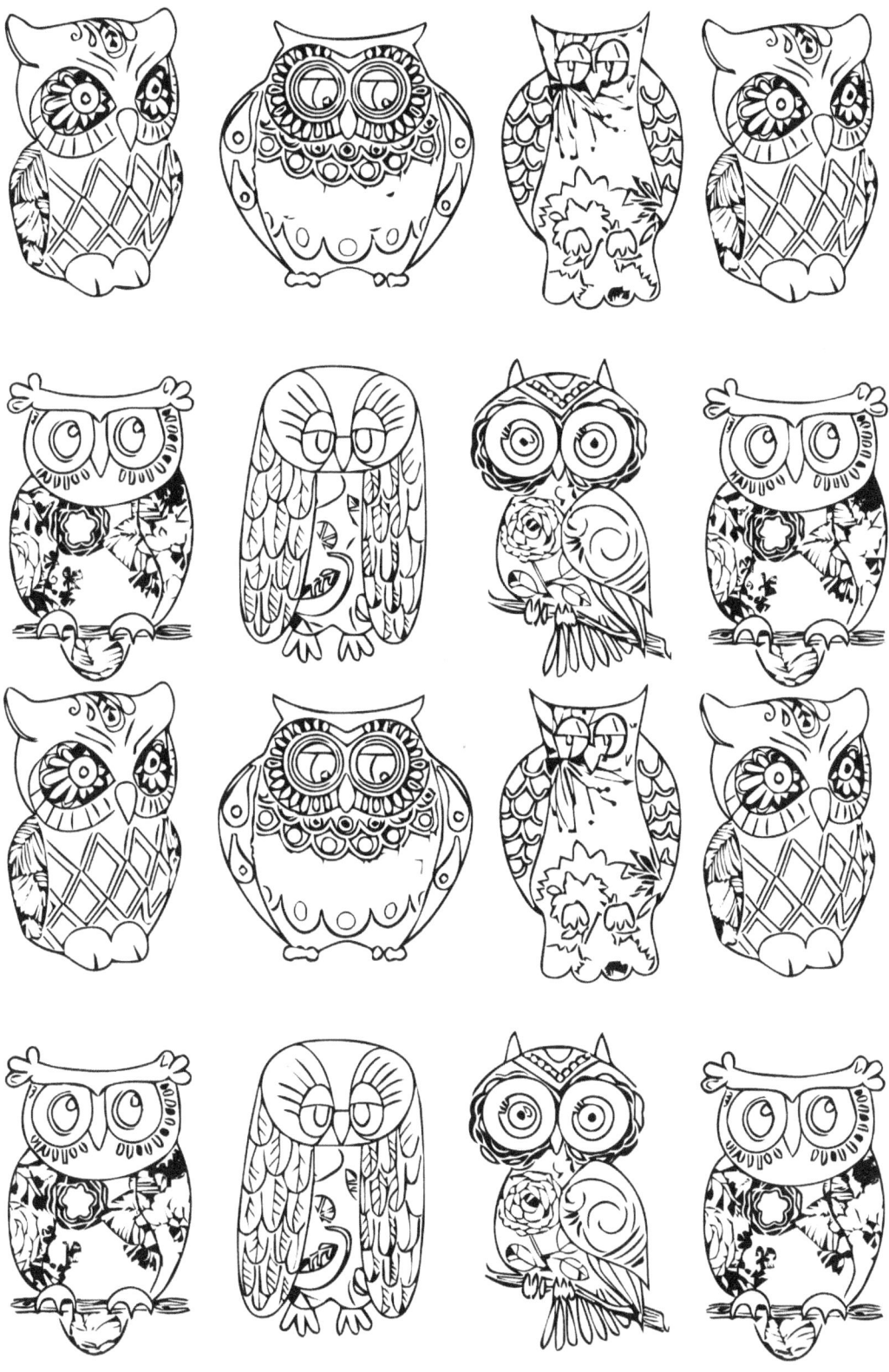

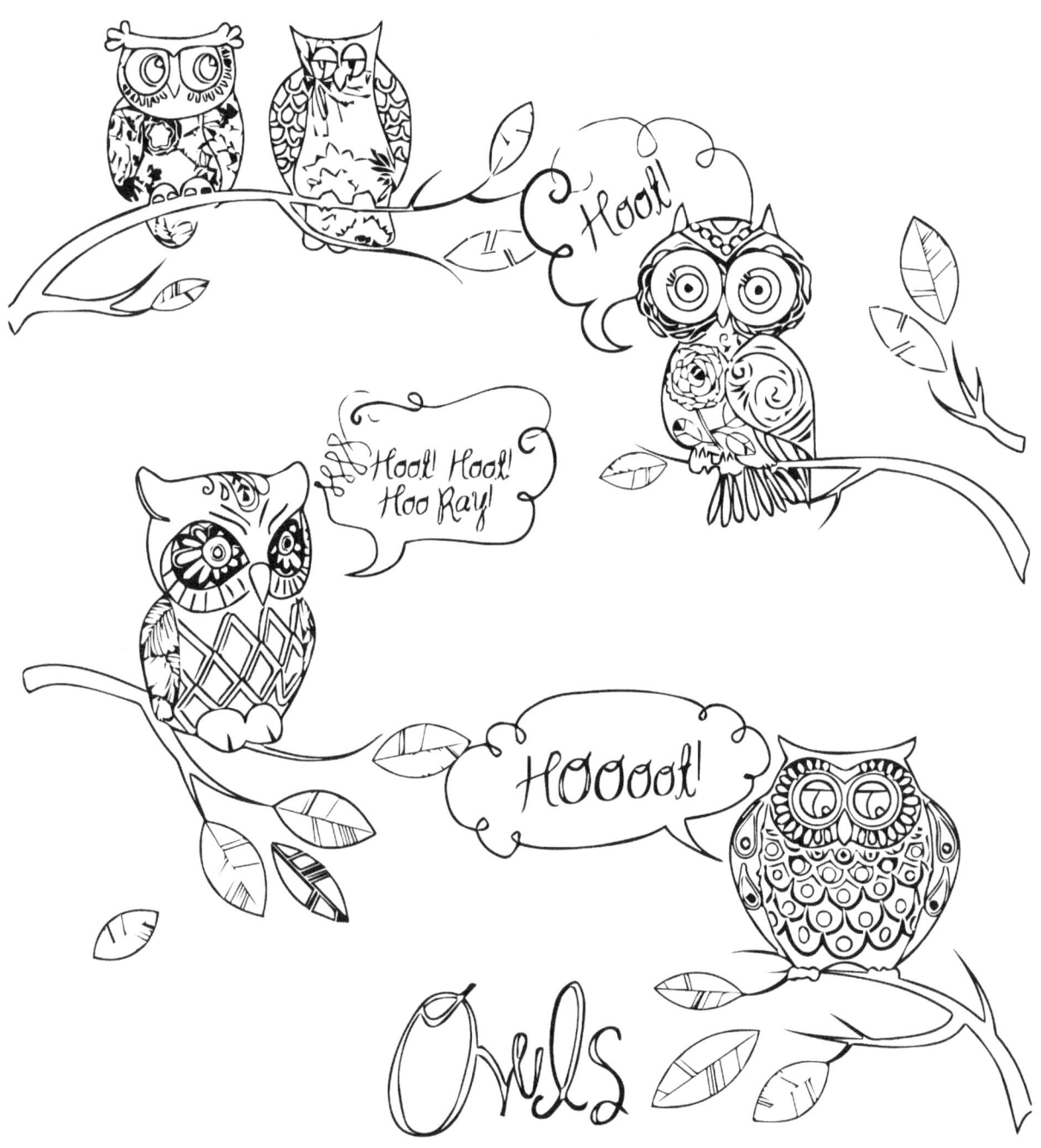

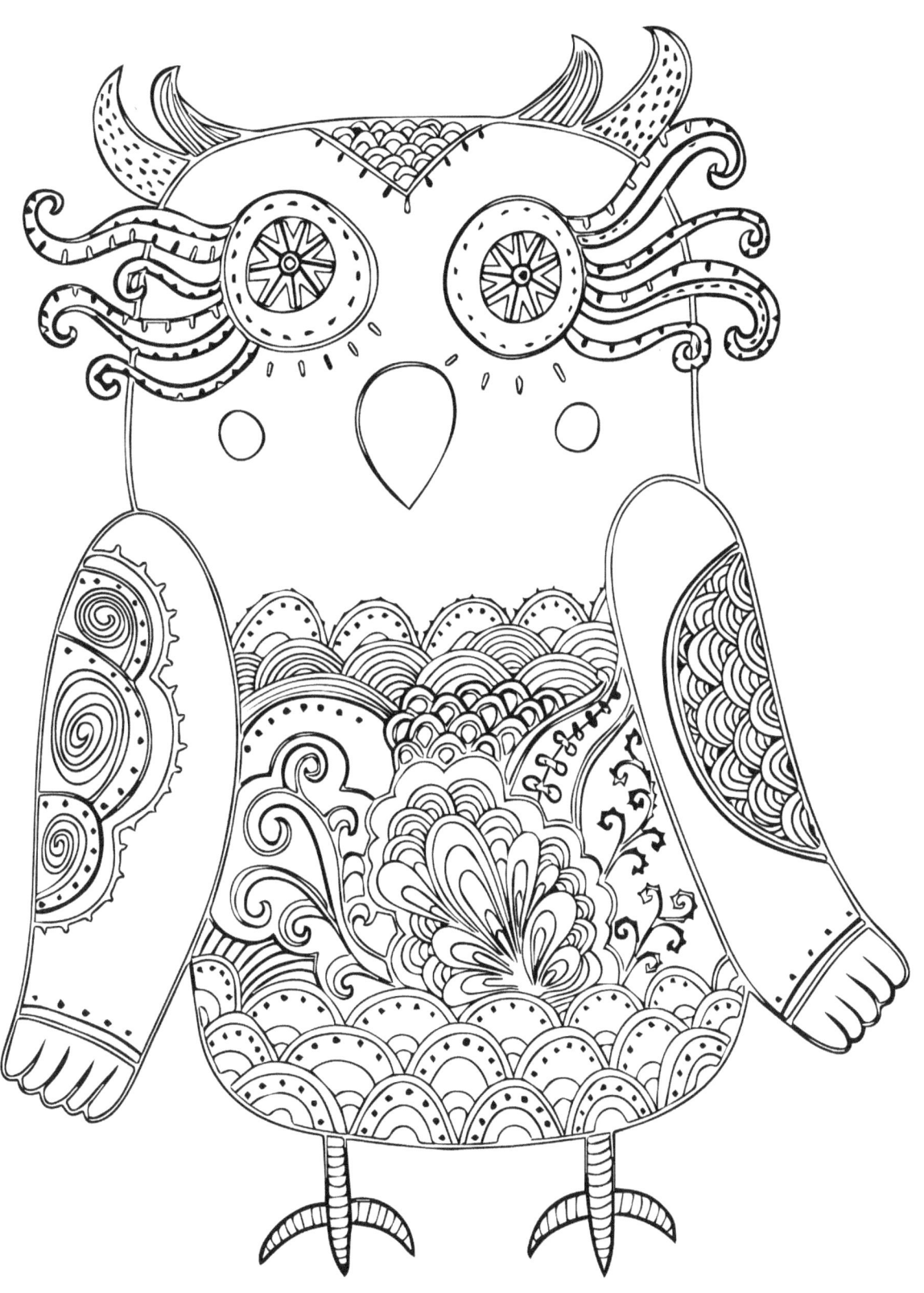

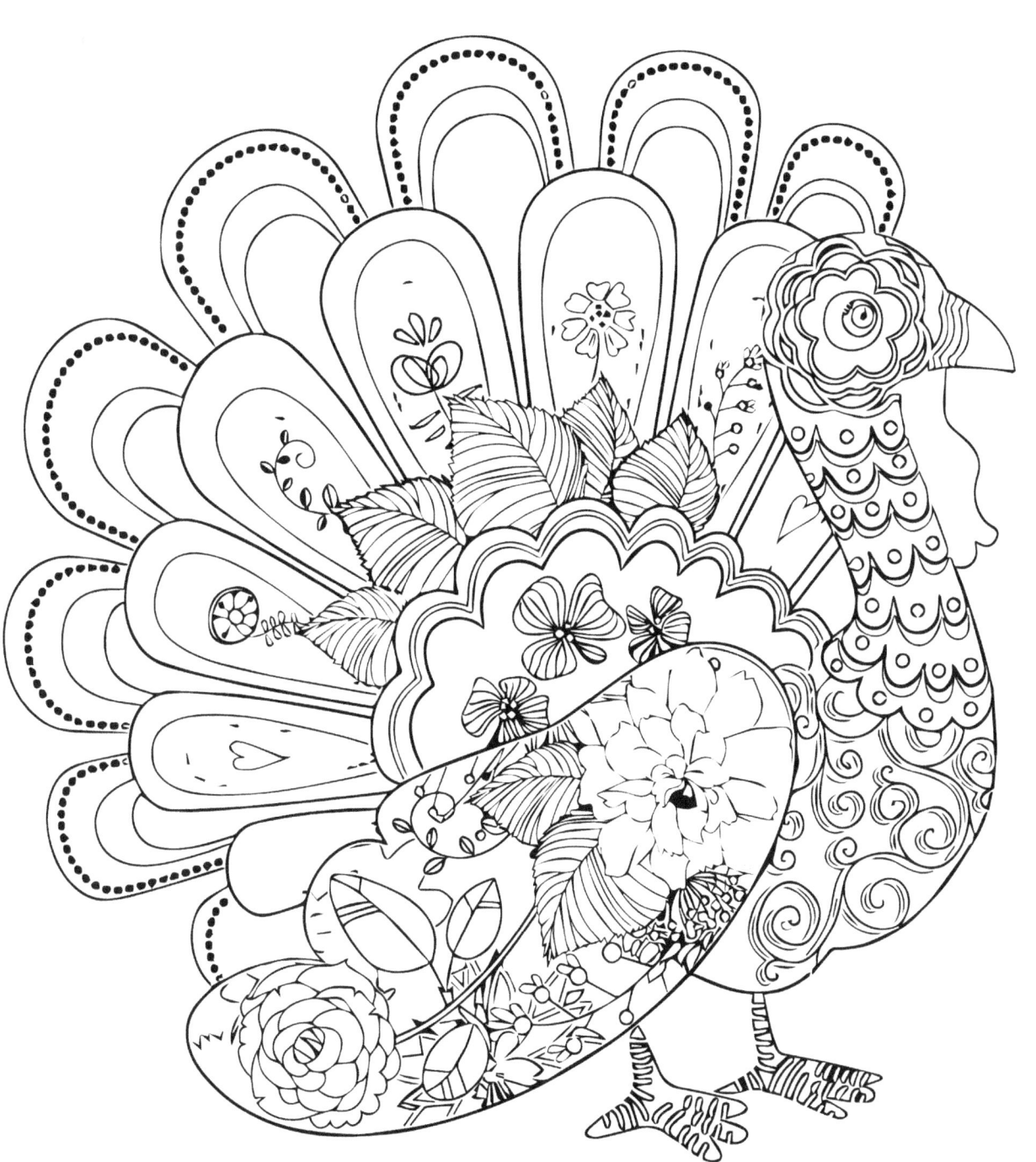

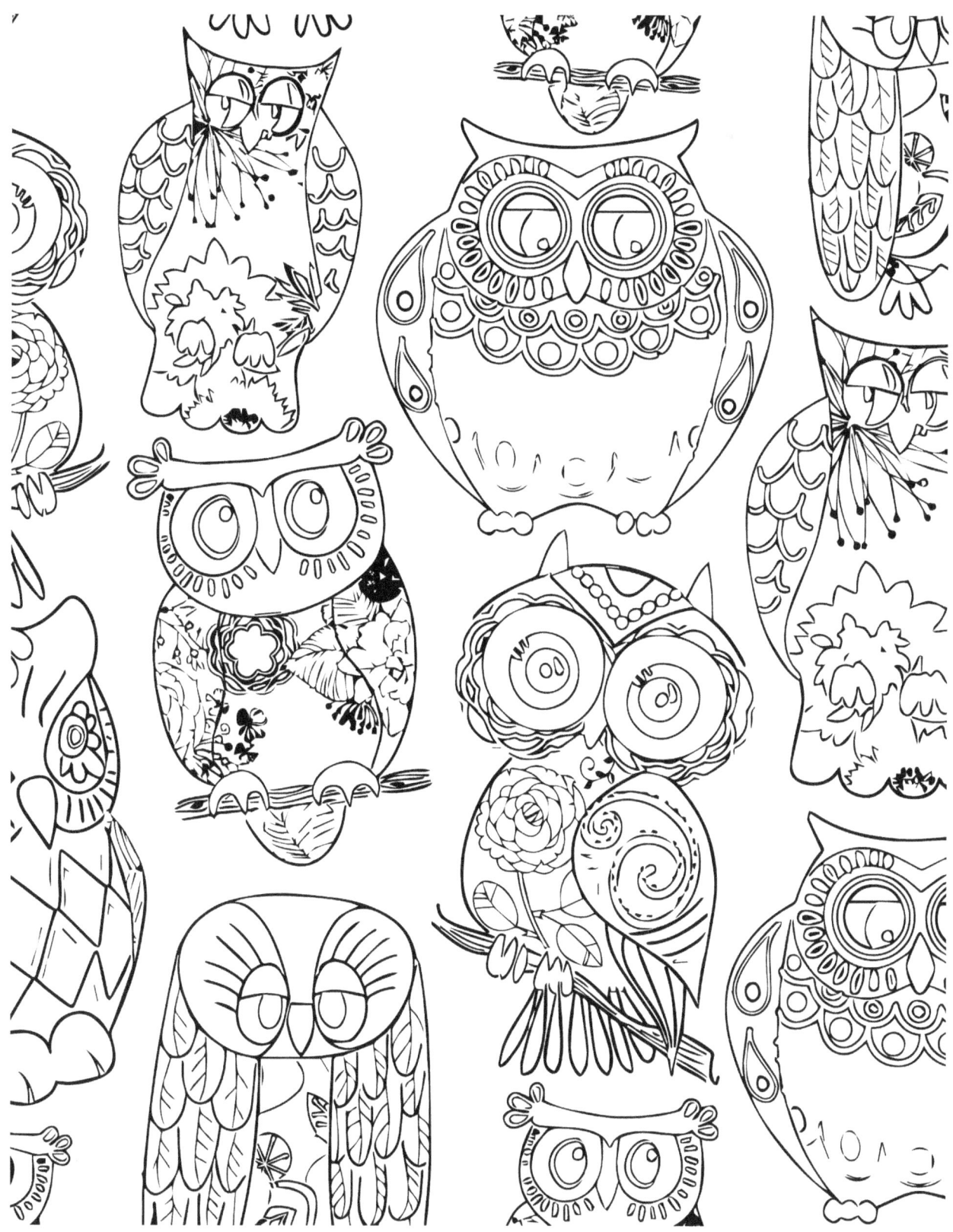

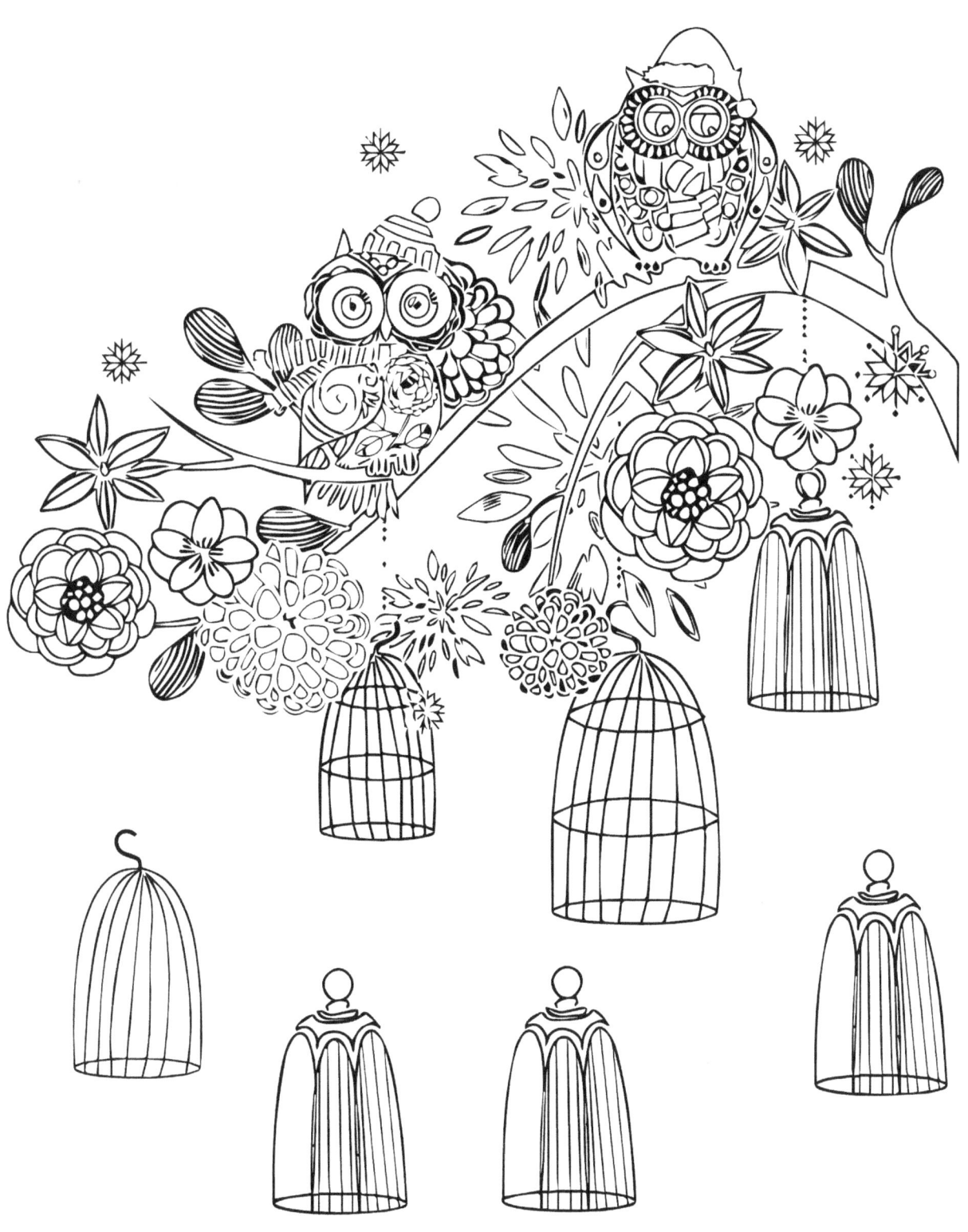

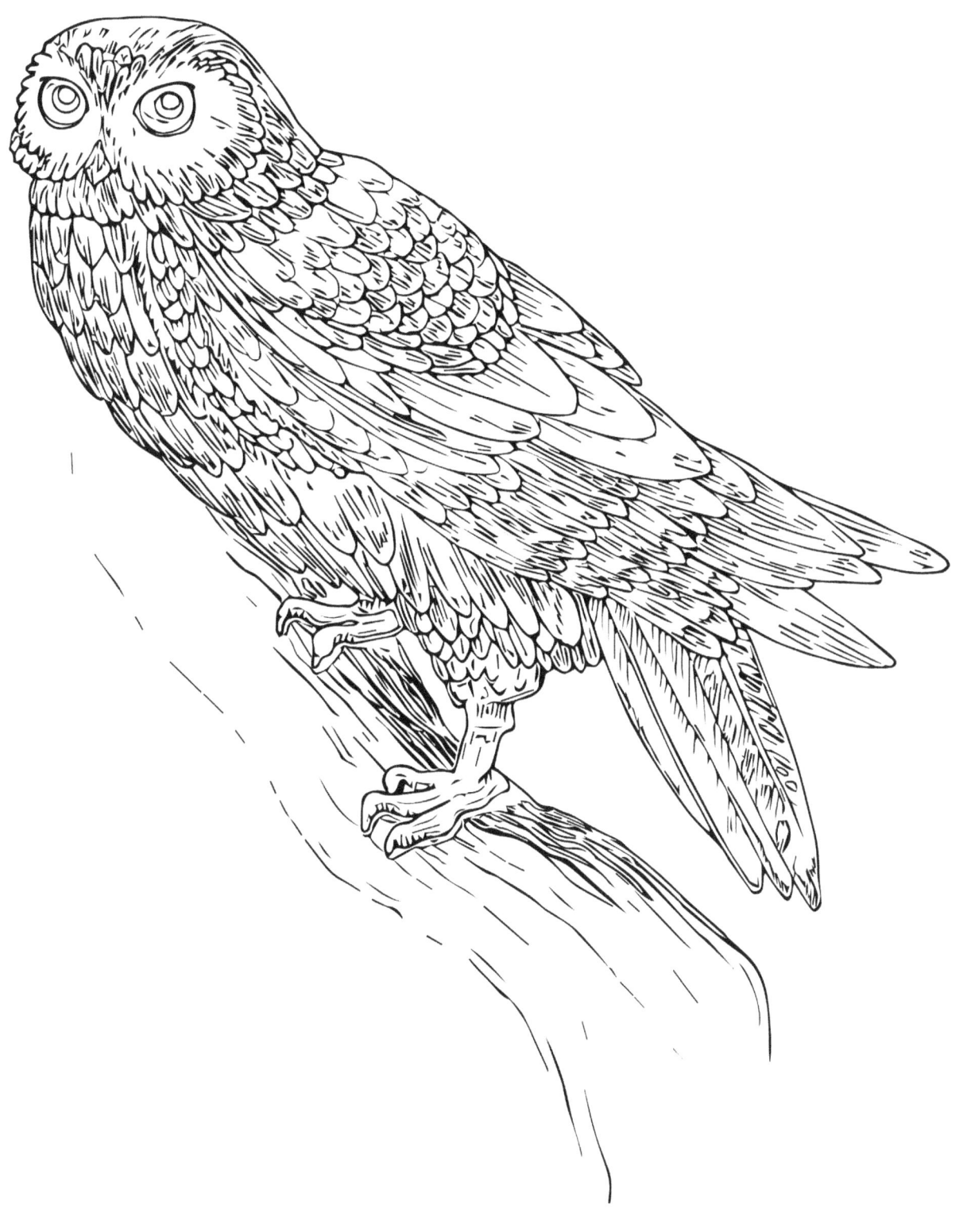

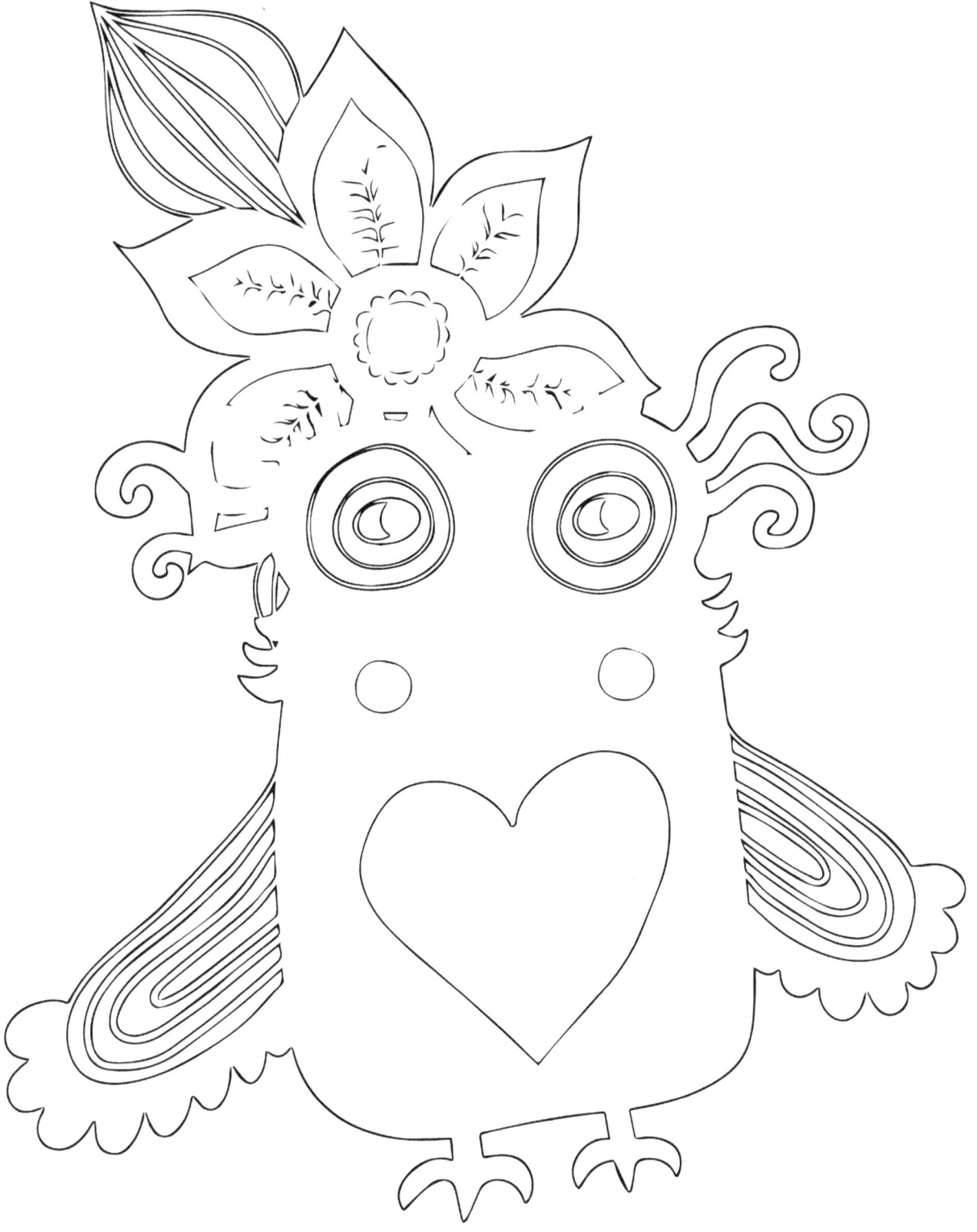

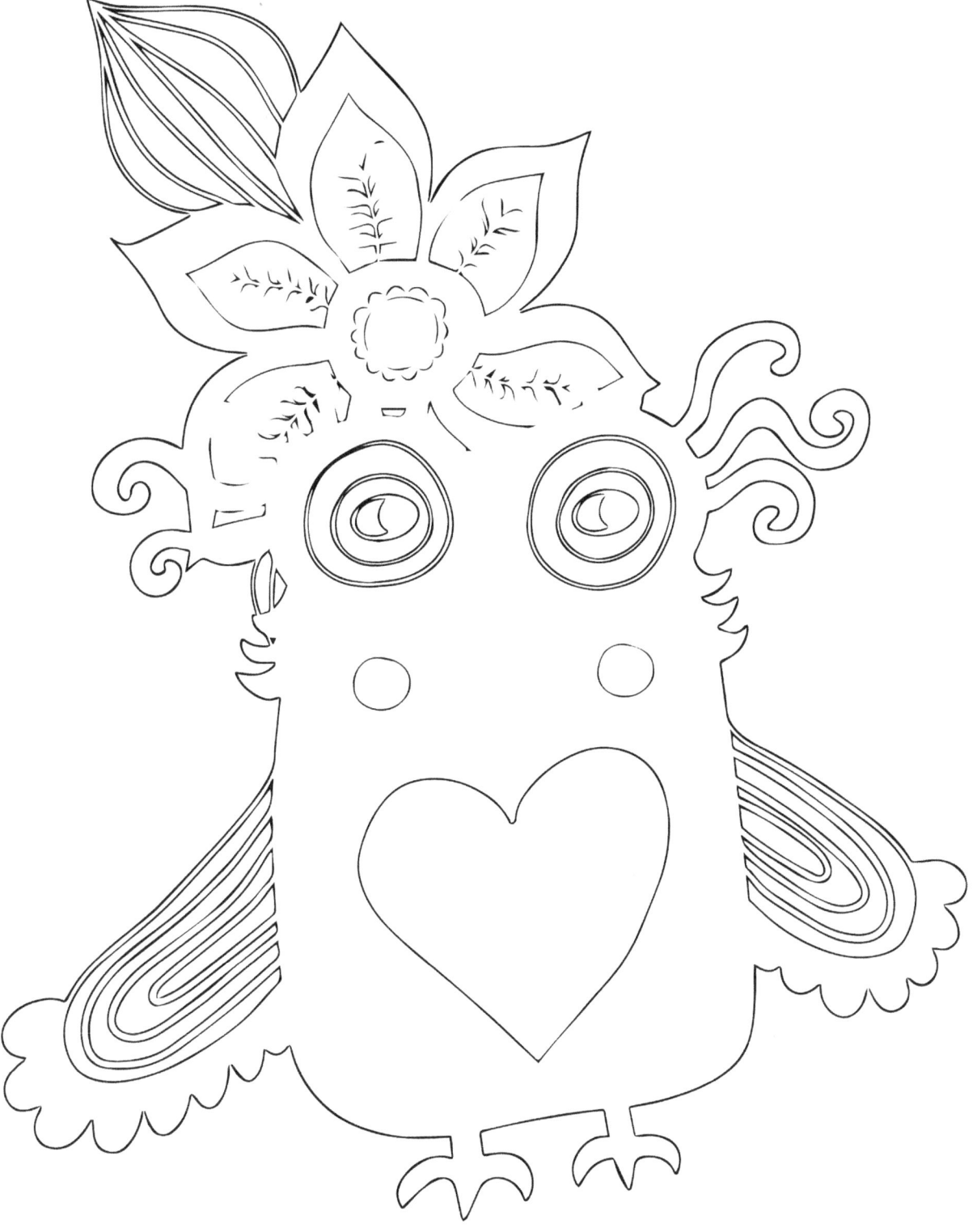

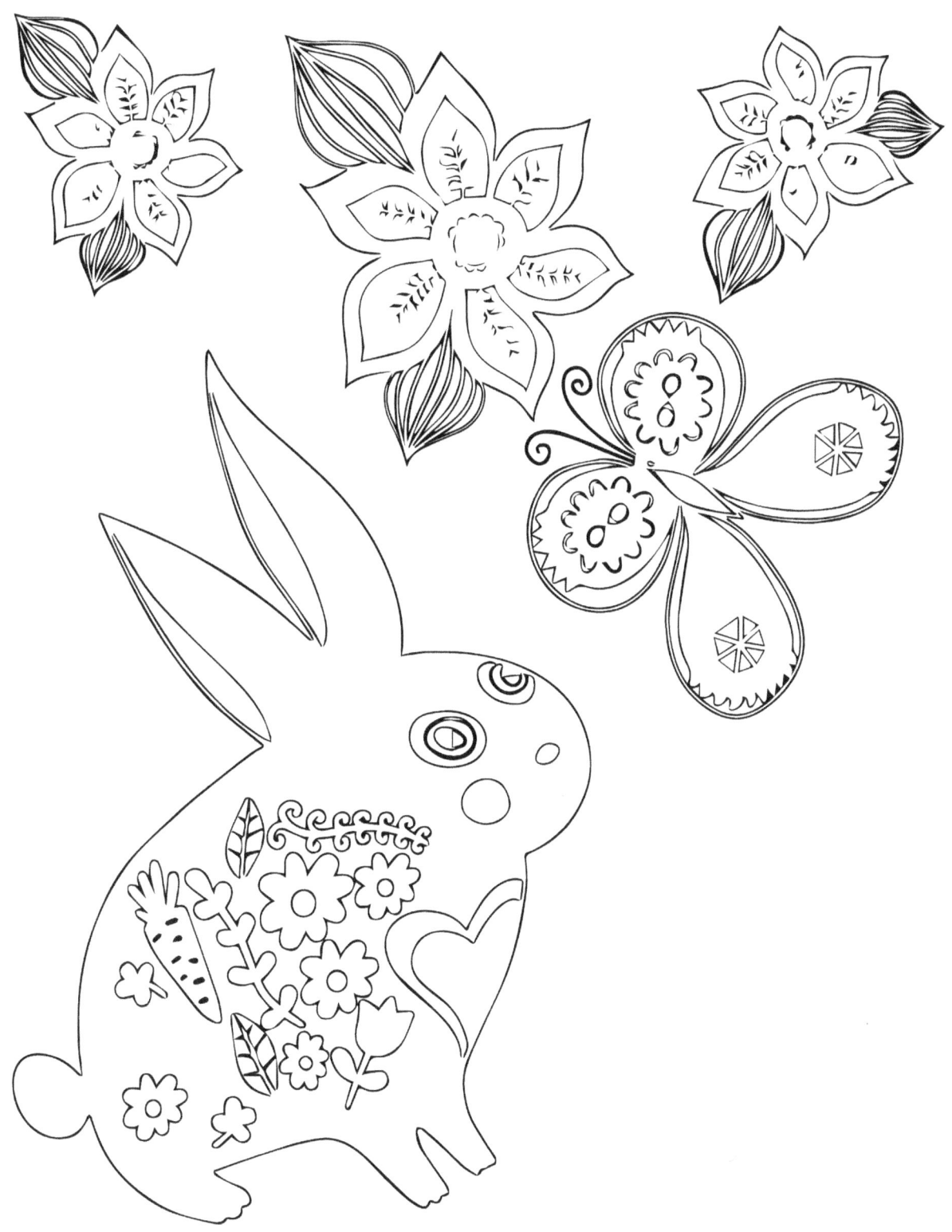

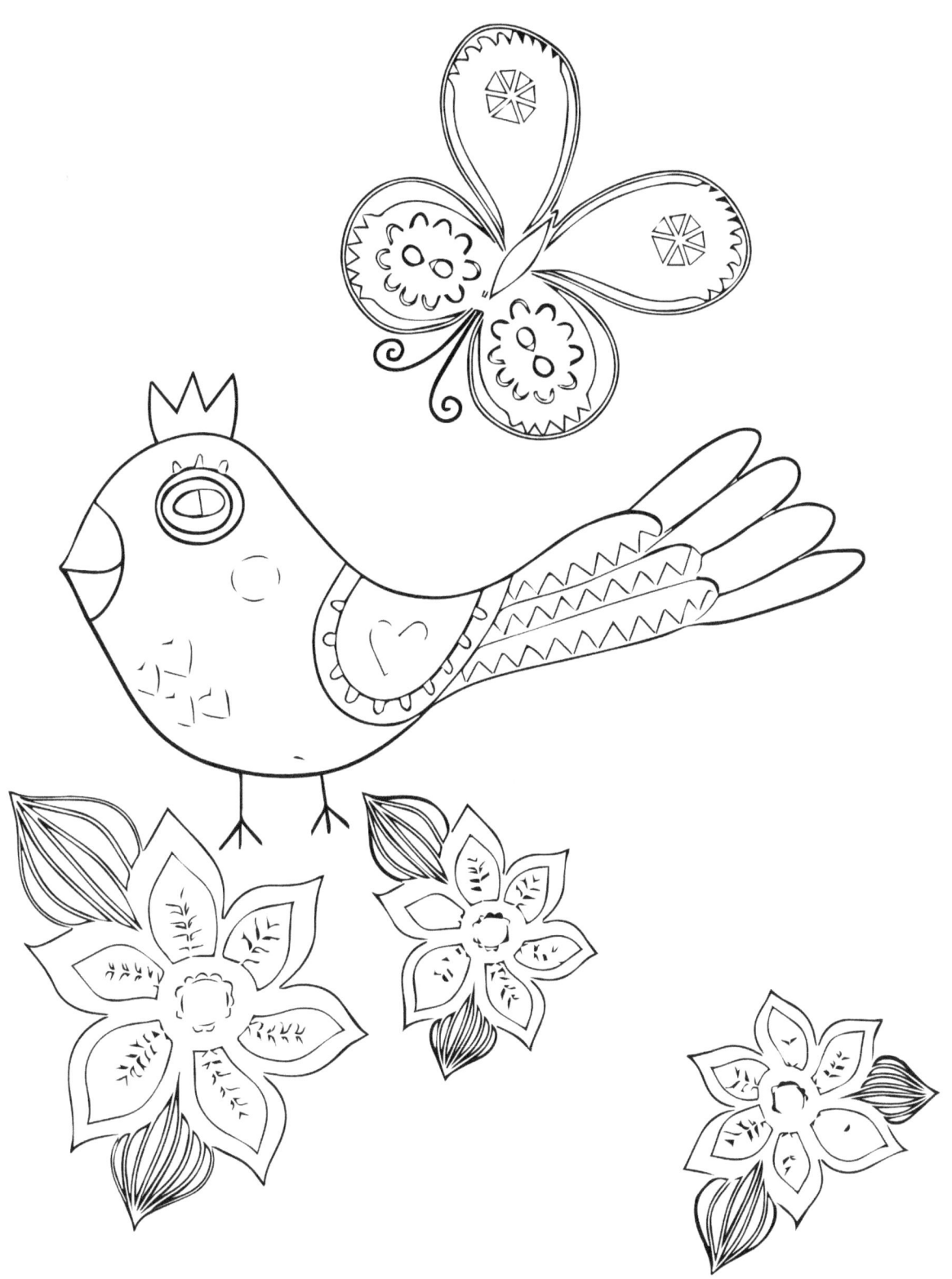

Thank You

Hope you've enjoyed your reading experience.

We here at Adult Coloring Book J. Kaiwell will always strive to deliver to you the highest quality guides.

So I'd like to thank you for supporting us and reading until the very end.

Before you go, would you mind leaving us a review on Amazon?

It will mean a lot to us and support us creating high quality guides for you in the future.

Thanks once again and here's where you can leave a review.

Warmly yours,
The Adult Coloring Book J. Kaiwell Team

www.ingramcontent.com/pod-product-compliance
Lightning Source LLC
Chambersburg PA
CBHW080638190526
45169CB00009B/3420